THE WHITE-WEST: A LOOK IN THE MIRROR

THE WHITE-WEST: A Look in the Mirror

David Andersson

Prologue by Peter Geffen &
Photos and Illustrations by
Rafael Edwards

Pressenza.com

Contents

Prologue

It is rare in our times to hear a radical voice that is neither strident nor violent, yet here is the distinguished and deeply committed humanist, David Andersson, providing just that. In a series of forceful and accurate analyses, Andersson challenges us to look in the mirror and be honest with ourselves. Tackling the most complex issue of our time, the historic responsibility of the "White" world for actions that have led directly to our contemporary moral crisis, he combines facts and opinion in a humble and quite noble attempt to help us change direction.

I met David over 20 years ago when he first came to work in (of all things) the technology department of The Abraham Joshua Heschel School in NYC that I founded in 1983. It was probably no accident of fate that brought him to the school named for the Rabbi whose friendship and shared values-commitment with Dr. Martin Luther King, Jr. remains legendary. Over the years David invited me to many events of the Humanist community in New York and he traveled with me to Israel/Palestine. I saw his "humanism" manifest in his openness and his personal morality and ethics reflected in his authentic compassion as evidenced in the essays that follow.

I share with David a radical critique of our times. I am envious of the imagination and conviction he commits to the written word. My own teacher (and maybe by now a little of David's as well) Rabbi Abraham Joshua Heschel put the challenge this way:

> "To be human is to be involved, to act and to react, to wonder and to respond....To live means to be at the crossroads. There are many forces and drives within the self. What direction to take is a question we face again and again. Who am I? A mere chip from the block of being? Am I not both the chisel and the marble? Being and foreseeing? Being and bringing into being?"

This book will be of great assistance to those already on the path of personal and then communal renewal. It is of even greater import to those at the crossroads. Only we can be the ones to be "bringing into being."

Peter A. Geffen, Founder
The Abraham Joshua Heschel School
Founder and President,
The KIVUNIM Institute

Preface

The project that eventually became this book started with George Floyd's death on May 25, 2020. Like many Americans, I was trying to get my head around that senseless killing -- wondering (again, and then again) how anything like this could take place today, more than 50 years after the U.S. Civil Rights movement.

As more and more Black people were interviewed on the news, invited on talk shows, and given space for op-ed pieces, I started to realize that there is little, in reality, that communities of colors can and should do at this time to resolve the innate racism of this country. Why should Black people be held responsible for transforming a situation they didn't create? Why, instead, don't we focus on the people who have created this situation in the first place?

When I say "the people," I am not speaking about the hard-to-miss racists who are easily identified, interviewed on CNN, and publicly shamed for their outdated attitudes. I am talking about a collective people, with a collective set of beliefs, whose lives take place within a collective structure that has, at a minimum, allowed for and maximally perpetuated this violence against those outside their group for centuries. These beliefs, these structures, were so entrenched in the world these people grew up in -- their formative social, cultural, and political landscape -- that it appears to them simply as "reality," similar to the natural world, and not as a structure that has been constructed and can, therefore, be un-constructed. This landscape continues to operate today through their actions (and inaction), even though the world around them has changed enormously. While many of these people live in the United States, the cultural landscape they are a part of is broader, and includes most white people who live in the developed world. Reflecting this racial and geographic intersection, I have chosen to call this collective the *White-West.*

This book is a collection of op-eds originally published during the last year by Pressenza. Each article looks at a different aspect of the White-West dynamic and how it plays out against other cultures. While the focus is mostly on political and social issues linked to current events, the White-West can also be seen in music, photography, cinema, and art (just look, for example, at how the term "primitive art" has been used to describe work not deemed as "sophisticated" as Western art, such as Native American, sub-Saharan African or Pacific Island art).

After the riots last summer, there was a lot of discussion and hope for political reform ("defund the police"); at the same time, then-President Trump was becoming even more extreme and increasingly playing the race card with white supremacists. It has become very clear that the 2016 election was not as much of a political operation as a racist backlash, a revenge for eight years of a "Black" Obama presidency. But now that the Democrats have taken the White House again, they can take their revenge, and in this way he game goes forward, two steps forward, two steps back. The Republicans say racism doesn't exist; the Democrats insist the answer is political and economic. Nothing changes, however, because the problem is deeper than that.

As an organizer for almost 40 years, I used to believe that if you just focused on the right campaign at the right time, change would come. I don't believe that anymore. Universal Humanism, the philosophy to which I ascribe, is based on the principle that profound social transformation is only achieved if simultaneously with profound personal transformation. Institutional racism and discrimination will not be overcome by political reform alone, but will also require an intentional transformation of our own formative landscape. The white community needs to relearn how to see the world and our place into it. We have to learn to recognize the old belief system that still operates in all of us, and have the courage to let it go, once and for all. It is a system that may have benefited our ancestors in the past, but it is certainly strangling our future now, as well as the future of the whole planet. Without this deep, honest, and uncomfortable work, nothing will truly change.

A note on tone: often in these articles I have relied on sarcasm and humor, not as a way of making light of these issues, but as a way of helping us to see the contradictions, inconsistencies, and ultimately, absurdity of of the White-West mentality. I hope no one takes offense.

Principle 8

"You will make your conflicts disappear when you understand them in their ultimate root, not when you want to resolve them."

from "The Inner Look"by Silo

75 Years Ago, the U.S. Destroyed Japanese Culture

08/09/2020

When the U.S. dropped a nuclear weapon on Nagasaki, just three days after having bombed Hiroshima, they knew exactly what the level of destruction would be and the extent of the humanitarian disaster. Less than a second after the detonation, the northern end of the city had been destroyed and 35,000 people had died.

Some might propose a political and military justification for Hiroshima, but why Nagasaki? Why a second nuclear bomb just three days later? We could also question why Japanese-American citizens were put in US concentration camps during the war, incarcerated in their own country by their own government.

The only real explanation that makes sense is that the U.S. wanted to ensure that the Japanese would forever be a sub-culture to the White-West. If you ask the Japanese why they were bombed, they will tell you it was because they were non-white. "Do you think the US would have used nuclear weapons against Nazi Germany?" they ask.

In just a few minutes the US achieved what took 400 years for the European countries who colonized Africa and South America to do. Japan is now a territorial extension of the U.S., hosts several American military bases, and plays a key role in the U.S.'s geopolitical game in Asia. The Armenian Genocide Museum defines cultural genocide as "acts and measures undertaken to destroy nations' or ethnic groups' culture through spiritual, national, and cultural destruction." Following this definition, August 9 was 5-second cultural genocide.

Every important event happening in today's world has a profound cultural aspect and we need to see this more closely. U.S. tension with China, Brexit, the election of Donald Trump, the Black Lives Matter movement, the coup in Bolivia to remove Evo Morales -- all of these and many more show the White-West forces in action. These issues can't just be justified economically; we need to recognize that underneath them lies the primitive fight for white cultural domination.

Beyond the White-West vs China Cultural Clash

08/16/2020

On July 22, the Texas Tribune reported that the Trump administration had ordered the closing of Houston's Chinese Consulate. The Chinese Government retaliated by closing the U.S. consulate in Chengdu, the capital of China's Sichuan province. Chengdu was an important diplomatic outpost for the U.S., covering a large swath of the country, including the controversial Tibetan Autonomous Region. Before these consulate wars, the biggest tension between the two countries had been over the 5G network, as Chinese telecom giants Huawei and ZTE now control about 40% of the global 5G infrastructure market. U.S. Attorney General William Barr, speaking at a conference in Washington, said that allowing China to establish 5G dominance was a "monumental danger," as Beijing could use the technology for monitoring and surveillance. "The stakes are far higher than that" Mr. Barr continued, as it was the first time in history that the United States was not the leader in a major technological sector that would underpin future innovation. This line, coming from the Attorney General of the supreme capitalist country in the world, is amazing. Isn't competition the idea of the game after all?

This situation, however, has more to do with culture than money. On one side we have what I call the White-West, which has been controlling most of the world for over two centuries by imposing its values, religion, and social and economic structures through violence in all forms. China, with four thousand years of civilization, has become the 2nd largest economic power in the world in only 20 years, taking leadership on new technology and green energy and partnering with over 70 countries on a New Silk Road initiative. There's no doubt that China is growing into a geopolitical heavyweight, stepping into the breach left by the United States on matters of free trade and climate change. "As some Western countries move backwards by erecting 'walls', China is contriving to build bridges, both literal and metaphorical," ran a recent commentary by Xinhua, a Chinese state-run media agency.

The dynamic between the two cultures has totally reversed — closed and introverted China has become more open and is looking to partner at the world level, while the White-West is closing its doors and becoming more enclosed, as seen in the UK by Brexit and in the U.S .by the Mexico wall, leaving the Paris agreement, quitting the WHO, and so on.

What is happening between the White-West and China will impact the future of humanity and therefore concerns us all. We cannot afford to enter into another Cold War, with tensions rising and countries around the planet being forced to choose a side. We have to find a way to move beyond cultural dominance — the pattern for thousands of years of human history — and into an era of cultural cohabitation and cooperation. It is a moment where every culture will have a part to play, but each will also need to be open to change. To move in this direction, there are few questions that need to be answered:

Can the White-West co-exist with other cultures as peers?

How could we animate other cultures, such as the indigenous, Muslim, Indian communities, to take on more of a leadership role?

What is it in my culture that needs to change to help the rest of humanity?

If there was a moment to fully implement the proposal of a Universal Human Nation, it would be right now. For this, we need to define well how cultures will interact and partner between each other. It not a question of money, markets or anything like that (these are secondary issues), but rather about having a strong image of a future where cultures understand, trust, work, and partner with each other and commit to resolve any conflict without the use of violence.

Getting Control of Belarus is a Big Deal for the White-West

08/21/2020

Every mainstream media outlet is covering the protests over the election results in Belarus. Could this be the new Ukraine? Maybe not, but it is definitely a continuation of attempts by the White-West's to get closer to Russia's border.

Just a few days ago, Deutsche Welle published "Pompeo signs deal to move US troops from Germany to Poland," which stated "The U.S. has signed a deal with Poland to begin the redeployment of American troops from Germany to the Eastern European country. The agreement," it went on, "also makes Poland the new headquarters of the US Army V Corps."

Looking at the map, we can understand the interest in Belarus' election results. Getting control of Belarus is a big deal for the White-West, which is using the rhetoric of "preserving democracy" to take advantage of the situation politically. They already have far-right governments in Hungary and Poland under their control.

The most troubling part is that there is little political opposition in the U.S. or Europe, on either the right or the left, to NATO's expansion to the Russian border, which would reduce Moscow's influence on the rest of the world and ensure the White-West's dominance.

How can we stop the bullying of the White-West? The answer is complicated, but here are a few important steps in that direction:

- close the World Bank and the International Monetary Fund (IMF);
- cancel external debts for all countries;
- reform the U.N. Security Council;
- pass the Treaty on the Prohibition of Nuclear Weapons (TPNW);
- remove foreign troops from occupied territories;
- use green technology to produce 80% of the world energy;
- close tax havens;
- implement Universal Basic Income (UBI);
- implement a maximum wage;
- remove U.S. and European economic sanctions against other countries; and
- shut down NATO.

Who is going to do all this? The White-West needs to do it, because they have created the problem and they have the power to fix it. They can't keep going to other cultures and offering humanitarian aid to fix problems they created in the first place (many of which, by the way, they are unable to deal with at home).

People from the White-West need to take the responsibility and leadership to transform their own culture, their own belief system, and their own economic system. It is time to look at themselves in the mirror and acknowledge what they have become: a monster incapable of satisfying the basic health, food, and housing needs of their own people.

It is not unlike the story of the guy who has tensions with his boss at work, and so after work goes to a bar, gets drunk, returns home and beats up his wife. All because he couldn't muster up the courage to talk to his boss.

Please, talk to your boss.

Greta the Great is Back

08/29/2020

On August 20, Swedish climate activist Greta Thunberg and three other teen activists had a 90-minute meeting with German Chancellor Angela Merkel to press their demands for tougher action to curb climate change. Germany currently holds the six-month rotating presidency of the European Union.

Greta, the 17 year-old environmental activist, is back to school and back in action, and this is a good news for all of us. Her courage and dedication are impressive. The 20th marked the second anniversary of the "Fridays for Future" school strikes she began in 2018, and youth are now taking part in these protests in over 150 countries. She has been motivating teenagers to educate their parents, asking them to go to the streets and make the adults face their contradictions and lack of courage. Thunberg understands very well that the climate change problem lies with the White-West: the United States, with just over 4%

of the world's population, is responsible for almost a third of the excess carbon dioxide that is heating the planet. The 28 countries of the European Union, taken as a group, come in just behind the United States in historical emissions.

Greta is one of the most humanist figures in the public eye today. She practices nonviolence, she organizes at the base, and she is very strategic. Her September 2019 speech at the United Nations earned enthusiastic praise from climate researchers, with many saying that in just a few years the 16-year-old had raised awareness of climate science and galvanized public support way beyond what they had been able to do in decades.

"I thought it was the most powerful speech I've ever seen," said Sally Benson, co-director of the Precourt Institute for Energy at Stanford University.

Greta knows how to push buttons. Politicians have bullied, insulted, and degraded her more forcefully than they did against those who created nuclear weapons. The insults are coming from the same people who got the U.S. to withdraw from the Paris Agreement.

We can only hope that Greta, along with this new generation of teenagers, will have the capacity to force the White-West to become a culture at harmony with nature: willing to share, replacing competition with cooperation, and placing the wellbeing of global humanity as a priority.

White Voters for Biden Political Action Front

09/11/2020

The boring 2020 U.S. presidential race is well under way, with just a few months left before its November finish. The main and maybe only real project of the Democratic Party is to kick Donald Trump out of the White House and keep him from taking a second term.

It is true that this election is important, but not for the reasons they sell to us. This election is important because things have to change profoundly and rapidly. We need to turn around the destructive direction our present-day society has taken. We need a strong cultural change, something like a nonviolent cultural revolution, and we should use this political space and the Biden candidacy to move our society forward and produce these much-needed transformations. The future of humanity is in question.

The main issue that engulfs everything else is violence and the use of it in all its forms: physical, economical, racial, sexual, religious, moral. This culture of violence is causing this crisis, and nothing is being done to stop it.

Here are just some of the ways this violence is being manifested:

- The United States, with just over 4% of the world's population, is responsible for almost a third of the excess carbon dioxide that is heating the planet, and the European Union, taken as a group, comes in just behind the United States. If we combine the US and Europe, the White-West is responsible for over 60% of the excess carbon dioxide.
- The concentration of capital, mainly by the white community, is producing a growing gap between rich and poor. African-Americans, for example, lost 40% of their small businesses during COVID, while Amazon and other tech behemoths saw their profits skyrocket. Today, the average white family has roughly 10 times the wealth as the average black family, and white college graduates have over seven times more wealth than Black college graduates.
- Militarization, nuclear weapons, and a disproportionate military budget are used by our country to bully the rest of humanity. Domestic police use military equipment to assault and kill people of color in the streets of U.S. cities and 36,000 Americans are killed by guns each year—an average of 100 per day.
- Our current formal democracy, which relies on a disconnected form of representation with minimal participation called voting, hasn't evolved much over the past two hundred years. Within this outdated system, there is outright disregard of voting rights, especially among communities of color. and immigrants In some neighborhoods in New York City, less than 50% of the population is eligible to vote.

The white community needs to stand up and take responsibility for the failures caused by the dominant values of competition and extreme individualism, which in turn have led to concentration of power and wealth, the use of violence as the primary way to resolve conflicts, and rampant discrimination against minority cultures and people of color.

If you take to the street for the freedom not to wear a mask, you have picked the wrong fight. The mask is not about YOU; like a driver's license, it is meant to stop you killing other people. The only real freedom you have is to liberate yourself from violence and contradiction, and to choose to begin treating others the way you want to be treated. You need to recognize that you currently have very little freedom in your own life. You didn't pick your primary language, you had very little choice about the work you are doing, and you probably didn't choose the God you believe in or the religion you belong to. You have no power over how your tax dollars are spent (mainly to kill people). You didn't choose the country you were born in. Have you ever questioned for a minute the type of sexual partner (gender) you are most comfortable with? You have one form of marriage, one economic system, one flag on your lawn.

Maybe now you see the need for us to make some intentional decisions. It is our job to tell our potential future employee, Joe Biden, what to do. We pay the President's salary with our tax dollars, so let's not waste it. Let's get out of our nihilism, learn from our mistakes, reconcile with our enemies, and stop the violence. Let's implement a Universal Basic Income. Let's ban nuclear weapons. Let's pay reparations to African-Americans. Let's reduce the US military budget by 10% in order to pay for green energy development. Let Biden know what his political program will be. Let's DO IT because without us nothing is going to change.

California: The Center of the White-West is Burning

09/12/2020

First, we need to send wishes for well-being to our brothers and sisters in California who are confronting an unprecedented disaster. The fires there are absolutely ferocious.

California is the biggest state in the country and is the world's fifth-largest economy, according to data released in May 2018 by the U.S. Department of Commerce. Its 2017 Gross State Product was $2.747 trillion, surpassing the United Kingdom's $2.625 trillion Gross Domestic Product.

These fires are not a natural disaster but are human made. California could have been a beacon of cultural and social transformation, harvesting the energy and dynamic of the 1960's social movements to orient society in a new direction: a balanced ecology, innovative and energy-smart public transportation system, new architectural avenues for public housing, a democratized economical structure, and increased access to direct democracy and expanded political participation through technology. California could have produced a whole new social model, as it had everything in its hands to do it — people, the coastline, sunshine, fertile land, and the support of the rest of the country.

Instead, California became the center of the System. Silo once elegantly described the System as "the center of the secondary," and in this California has become the perfect model. Somewhere California took a wrong turn and became the center of individualism, capitalism, materialism, and immediatism. Party as if there's no tomorrow.

But now tomorrow has come, and this American Dream has become a nightmare. Climate change is very real, and California has done little about it. It is not a question of left or right, Republican or Democrat, but one of culture. Having two or three cars per family is the norm, public transportation is devalued, and making money is the priority (there are currently 170 billionaires in California alone).

So now what? The same opportunities exist in California today as they did 60 years ago. The issue is what model to choose, what values to prioritize, and what project toward the future to launch? Are we really going to humanize this world or just pretend to do it? Will we start working together — private, public, local, national, international — for real collaboration and solidarity, with the understanding that my freedom must not infringe someone else's freedom? Can we all agree to ban the use of violence to resolve conflicts, that science should be accepted as our ultimate knowledge, that money and economy must be at the service of humanity and social development (and not the reverse), that there is nothing more important that our fellow human beings and their wellbeing? If we learn to treat people well, we will treat nature and the animal kingdom well too.

We can only hope that these fires will burn through the illusions about our present society and open minds and hearts. We must all become active in the current of humanization that has been working for over 50 years with the same proposals: to put personal development at the same level as social development (there is not one without the other); to treat others as you want to be treated; to prioritize reconciliation over revenge; to oppose violence in all its forms and to take part in nonviolent movements that have saved humanity many times over (in India, the US, Ireland, South Africa, and much more places). The decisions we make now will have repercussions for generations to come.

The Stages of Death for the White-West

09/20/2020

Everyone is trying to make sense of this current moment of almost total chaos. Some call it anarchy, but that is not correct as we still have governance at many levels. This state of chaos can be seen in many situations: with the climate crisis (forest fires, storms, floods, air pollution, record temperatures); in politics, where each clan tries to undo anything the other did or proposed, both clans without any project toward the future; socially, where urban downtowns are becoming centers of unrest, protest, and shootings, with stores closed and boarded up; in health, where a pandemic unmasks a dysfunctional society, incapable of responding to the most basic needs of its population; and, finally, in the economy, where the rich take advantage of this human tragedy to become even wealthier, and those with the lowest income become even poorer and approach homelessness. The toll has been unprecedented. Prevalence of depression in the US has increased more than 3-fold during the COVID-19 pandemic, from 8.5% to 27.8%.

A few weeks ago, the Hudson Valley Park of Study organized an online discussion titled "Accompanying People as They Approach Death," in which Victor Piccininni, author of the book *The Art of Accompaniment: Tools and Practices for Personal and Spiritual Accompaniment in Palliative Care and End-of-Life,* spoke about three stages in a dying process. "The first stage is called Chaos," Piccininni said, "and its most significant indicators are denial, internal and external struggle, fear, anger, isolation, depression, internal and external violence. It is the irrational fear of losing the superficiality of the self and the body. "Stage Two," he continued, "is called arrival of the 'departure'. It is a surrender, a giving up of control, where the registers of peace, serenity, well-being begin to appear. The third stage is Reconciliation and Transcendence, where we see registers of deep inner peace and reconciliation with life."

Piccininni's description of the "chaos" stage fits perfectly with the current moment. It seems that society, as we know it, is dying. We are experiencing the disintegration of the White-West, and we witness daily expressions of the fear of loss of control. Not every culture is in this moment of process, but we can clearly see the West is facing it. If we are interested in accompanying this process, we need to help our culture get to Stage Two and accept that the White-West is losing its domination. The White-West culture will no longer be the one-and-only reference and center of prestige. The current stage of chaos could get much worse, leading to violence and war, or it could slowly shift to Stage Two, depending on how we act.

It is difficult for us to accept that someone close is dying and that we have to let them go. Sometimes, we take extraordinary measures to try to keep that person alive, even if they were a total jerk.

Everyone knows that the White-West culture is dying, from the white supremacists on the right to those on the extreme left. The only question is, are we in the right disposition to accompany the process through Stage Two and towards Stage Three, Reconciliation and Transcendence? Can we build a new civilization, a Universal Human Nation, where nations operating with diverse social structures will come together to share, support, and learn from one another? As Piccininni says, accompaniment is an art, and maybe one we will need to learn very quickly.

Latinx Voters for Biden Political Action Front

09/28/2020

After writing "White Voters for Biden Political Action Front" a few weeks ago, Javier Castaño, director of Queens Latino, asked if I could do an article about the importance of the Latinx vote in the 2020 U.S. presidential election.

This coming election is a cultural fight between a Republican who is trying the reenforce the supremacy of the white culture and a neoliberal Democrat.

We have to remember that Trump was elected as a backlash to the presidency of Barack Obama, as a big chunk of the white community didn't like having a Black president. From Day One, Trump's agenda was to destroy everything done during the previous administration. This same thing happened in South America, with Bolsonaro reversing advancements made by Lula/Rousseff in Brazil, and, in Colombia, with Duque Márquez following Santos.

In the U.S., the real fight has not yet started, but this election might just be what lights the fire. The challenge will be to produce a nonviolent cultural revolution that will transform the current hegemonic society into a real multicultural community. This transformation would have repercussions far beyond the U.S. border, and could potentially transform a large part of the world.

We have all seen atrocious images of Latinx families being separated while under ICE custody and small children being kept in cages. We have also seen caravans from Central America being stopped at the Mexican border, placing those migrants at the mercy of local cartels. These actions were meant to produce fear and show the Latinx community that they are not welcome in the U.S. It is the same racist tactics that have been used in the past against Blacks.

A hindrance to this transformation is the illusion, held by some people, that Latinos can become "white" and integrate into the culture of power. That has not and will not happen. For the White-West, it does not matter if you are Colombian, Chilean, or Mexican, you speak Spanish (or Portuguese) and that is enough to make you "other."

If we have learnt one thing from the Coronavirus pandemic, it is that the system in the U.S. is different for people of color than for the white community. When adjusted for age, Black and Latinx Americans were 3.3 times more likely to die from COVID than their white neighbors.

This presidential campaign should force any American who comes from south of the U.S. border to recognize themself as Latinx. The Blacks understood it very early in their fight and instilled pride in the cultural identity of being Black.

It is almost impossible for Biden to win this election without winning the Black and Latinx vote. Biden cannot be expected to unite existing political divisions in the Latinx community between left/right, socialism/capitalism, etc., but, in reality, those divisions have very little to do with this election. Both major candidates are capitalist, neoliberal, militarist. But one is also clearly antihumanist, antidemocratic, nationalistic, and deeply committed to preserving the dominant white culture. Another four years would further deepen divisions within the country, and poison relations with people around the world.

Imagine for a minute a "LATINXS FOR BIDEN" movement uniting millions of Latin-Americans, from Cuba to Chile, with one objective only: to openly confront discrimination in the U.S. in all its forms. Everything else would fall in place after that. This is not the moment to form subdivisions like "Colombians for Biden." Biden does not have a specific project for each country of Latin America and, besides, this is not the issue.

This is a crucial moment for Latin-Americans. Do they want their culture to be a subculture of the White-West? Can they instead help lead us on a new course, and launch an image of the future that is based on the best qualities and values of their own rich culture? This election is about choosing to go in a new direction, connecting to what people in their hearts know is the only coherent choice for humanity's future. Voting for Biden is just a small step in that incredible journey, but it's an important one to take.

October 2nd a Nonviolence Day in the White West

10/02/2020

This year, it's complicated in this part of the world to hold a joyful celebration of nonviolence. October 2, the International Day of Nonviolence, is meant to be a celebration of Gandhi's birthday and an opportunity to commemorate the work of many others who have advanced nonviolent conflict resolution, opposed systemic discrimination, built a culture of peace, and fought against the destruction of humanity's habitat.

The mainstream media will be not be covering this day, since corporate media makes large profits from reporting violence and bias. There will be no #nonviolence trending on Twitter, no special debate in Congress. Joe Biden will not be announcing plans for developing nonviolence curricula for kindergarten through college. CEOs won't be unrolling a strategy to reinvest their corporation's money to serve the community at large. And we probably won't see the police addressing entrenched discrimination against communities of color and talking about how to stop being hyper-militarized agents who beat and kill people on the street.

We have, however, seen some opportunist politicians asking protestors — after seeing the killing of their brothers by police — to organize nonviolently, without themselves first condemning the immoral and disproportionate use of violence by the police. It seems nonviolence for them is to be used only by minorities fighting against a violent system (that created the problem at the first place).

Today, we recognize the power of transformation offered by nonviolence. Nonviolence has transformed countries, changed the face of continents, and provided a cultural identity to discriminated communities. We are, perhaps, facing the total collapse of this violent system we live in. Building a new culture of nonviolence is the only real option for the future of the human race.

In closing, here are few words from Silo, an Argentinian nonviolence leader, extracted from one of his most important speeches, "The Healing of Suffering," given in Punta de Vacas, Argentina on May 4, 1969:

"There are other forms of violence that are imposed by the Philistine morality. You wish to impose your way of life upon another; you wish to impose your vocation upon another. But who has told you that you are an example that must be followed? Who has told you that you can impose a way of life because it pleases you? What makes your way of life a model, a pattern that you have the right to impose on others? This, then, is another form of violence.

"Only inner faith and inner meditation can end the violence in you, in others, and in the world around you. All the other doors are false and do not lead away from this violence. This world is on the verge of exploding with no way to end the violence! Do not choose false doors. There are no politics that can solve this mad urge for violence. There is no political party or movement on the planet that can end the violence. Do not choose false doors that promise to lead away from the violence in the world... I have heard that all over the world young people are turning to false doors to try to escape the violence and inner

suffering. They turn to drugs as a solution. Do not choose false doors to try to end the violence.

"My brother, my sister, keep these simple commandments, as simple as these rocks, this snow, and this sun that bless us. Carry peace within you and carry it to others. My brother, my sister—if you look back in history, you will see the human being bearing the face of suffering. Remember, even as you gaze at that suffering face, that it is necessary to move forward, and it is necessary to learn to laugh, and it is necessary to learn to love.

"To you, my brother and sister, I cast this hope—this hope of joy, this hope of love—so that you elevate your heart and elevate your spirit, and so that you do not forget to elevate your body."

European Union and U.S. at War against Refugees and Immigrants

10/10/2020

During an interview with Pressenza, Marie Dutrepon described the unbearable day-to-day conditions in the Moria (Lesvos) concentration camp in Greece, a refugee camp designed for 2500 people that now hosts 25,000. She spoke of the risks for women going to the bathroom at night. Most astonishing was her description of the institutionalized physiological torture carried out by the European Union against the refugees.

"When I was there, we were about 6 lawyers for, at the time, 7-8,000 people," she said. " So there is not enough to prepare people properly. And there is no assistance. Here in Belgium, when someone applies for asylum, I accompany him to his hearing. Over there, it was almost impossible; there is no authorization, foreign lawyers are not allowed to accompany them, etc. Everything is so problematic at all levels. There is really nothing that goes, whether it be in

terms of information, transmission of information, clarity... even for lawyers specialized in asylum law, we often understood nothing, the ability of the rules that change all the time..."

Listening to this interview I was shocked by the similarities between the techniques and strategies used by the European Union at Moria and those used by ICE in the U.S. How is it that these two different political structures have developed and applied the same immoral actions against asylum seekers coming from war-torn and violent regions? These are two different political systems with very different structures and legal processes.

We have all seen the images of Latinx families being separated by ICE and the children locked in cages. We have seen caravans from Central America being stopped at the Mexican border, their riders placed at the mercy of local cartels. We have seen migrants and refugees becoming shipwrecked in the Mediterranean Sea in a desperate attempt to flee violence in their homes. *"If we do not intervene soon, there will be a sea of blood,"* said Carlotta Sami, spokeswoman for the UN refugee agency, UNHCR, in Italy.

The E.U. could easily have placed economic sanctions against the U.S for its human rights violations, and the U.S. could have done the same against the E.U.. Of course, neither happened, yet both, strangely, have continued their sanctions against Russia, Iran, and Venezuela.

This situation is only possible coming from a cultural mindset in which white people believe that they are the center of the universe and can do whatever they please, disregarding all international law. Their immigration strategies are based on discrimination and racism. Many countries in the world are accepting refugees at a proportion far beyond what the "White-West" has. Bangladesh, for example, one of the world's poorest countries, has accepted more refugees proportionately than France, Belgium, the U.S., Norway, Finland, Netherlands, Spain, Hungary, Portugal and Ireland (if you want to see details go to Cato.org.)

In truth, it goes far beyond a simple case of discrimination or racism. It displays a deep belief that the White-West has rights above any other culture, and is therefore free to use any justification it wants (democracy, human rights, free trade, free speech) to impose itself. It has been so deeply ingrained in our culture, for thousands of years, that it has become somewhat complicated to see it from the inside — like a fish who does not question the water in which it lives. We don't see that it's inhuman to cage children in camps, it's inhuman to empty a pistol into someone else's back, it's inhuman to keep using forms of energy that destroy our own environment, it's inhuman to keep access to economic resources from the majority of people just to satiate an unmanageable capitalist monster.

Europe and the U.S. need to accept asylum seekers and we need to treat them well. We need to do something in our heads and hearts and transform an uncomfortable situation into a valid action. This transformation could open our horizon to a new set of beliefs and values, not based on fears but on experiences of meaningful actions done well.

This is What We Really Need. ASAP

10/21/2020

Our "modern" society is facing many challenges, every one as important as the next: the environment, economy, violence, health, education, security, energy, food, concentration of capital, unemployment, etc. While it seems every politician knows exactly how to solve these problems, and has a unique plan to do so, very few people believe them anymore (for good reason). And so a crisis of distrust grows day by day. How did we get so disoriented? When did we lose our compass?

Ask your friends a very simple question -- "What do you *truly* need?" -- and notice how long it takes them to answer. How could we really live a harmonious life without knowing and thinking about our fundamental needs?

Among the practices of Silo's Message, there is a ceremony called "The Service" that elicits a connection with one's internal energy (force). At the close of the experience, participants are asked to reflect: "With this Force that we have received, let us concentrate our minds on the fulfillment of what we truly need..." In his first public speech, called "*The Healing of Suffering,*" Silo told the story of a rider's journey, which ends with this paragraph: "*At daybreak he sacrificed the cart of Desire. It is true that when he did so he lost the wheel of Pleasure, but then he also lost the wheel of Suffering. And so, abandoning the cart of Desire, he mounted the animal called Necessity and galloped on its back across the green fields until he reached his destiny.*" (See below for the complete story.)

That ceremony and that talk are meant to help us think about what we really *need,* not about what we want or desire. In our culture, it's easier to know what we desire than to know what we need. After all, our society is set up to sell us what we want but *don't* need. It is the magic of this system; we have shops, services, websites, politicians, banks, etc., ready to respond to our craziest desires. But how many people get what they want and are happy? How many people feel that they don't have enough and should have more?

Dr. Robert Lustig, in his book "*The Hacking of the American Mind,*" explains the scientific difference between pleasure and happiness, shows the consequences of our pursuit of pleasure, and links it to addiction, depression and chronic disease.

If we had a chance to transform our culture, based on our understanding and our experiences, we might start by meditating on this simple phrase: "*Let us concentrate our minds on the fulfillment of what we truly need...*". Imagine building a new society where everyone works together towards the fulfillment of what we truly need... from the personal to the communal to the global. It would make everything so much easier, more profound, and much more meaningful.

As the proverb says, "*Necessity is the mother of invention.*" So, let's invent something together! How about a real democracy, one focused on organizing active citizen participation in the construction of a society based on the fulfillment of what we all truly need. Isn't it better than drowning in this egocentric, pretentious, formal democracy manipulated by the selfish interest of a small minority?

——-———-———

I would like to tell you a story that took place long ago.

There was once a traveler who had to undertake a long journey. He yoked his animal to a cart and began the journey to his faraway destination, a journey he had to complete within a certain length of time. He called the animal Necessity and the cart Desire; one wheel of the cart he called Pleasure, and the other he called Pain. Our traveler turned his cart sometimes to the right and sometimes to the left, yet he never ceased moving toward his destiny. The faster the cart traveled, the faster turned the wheels of Pleasure and Pain, carrying as they did the cart of Desire and connected as they were by the same axle.

But the journey was very long, and after a time our traveler grew bored. So he decided to decorate his cart, and he began to adorn it with all manner of beautiful things. But the more he embellished the cart of Desire with these ornaments, the heavier became the load for Necessity to pull. On the curves and steep hills of the road, the poor animal grew too exhausted to pull the cart of Desire. And where the road was soft, the wheels of Pleasure and Suffering became mired in the earth.

One day, because the road was long and he was still very far from his destination, our traveler grew desperate. That night he decided to meditate on the problem, and in the midst of his meditation he heard the neighing of his old friend, Necessity. Comprehending the message, he arose very early the next morning and began to lighten the cart of its burden, stripping it of all its fine adornments. Then he set off once more toward his destination, with the animal Necessity pulling the cart at a brisk trot. Still, our traveler had already lost much time—time that was now irrecoverable. The next night he sat down again to meditate, and he realized, thanks to another message from his old friend, that now he had to undertake a task that was doubly difficult because it involved his letting go.

At daybreak he sacrificed the cart of Desire. It is true that when he did so he lost the wheel of Pleasure, but then he also lost the wheel of Suffering. And so, abandoning the cart of Desire, he mounted the animal called Necessity and galloped on its back across the green fields until he reached his destiny.

Letter of Support to the 5th Latin-American Humanist Forum

11/14/2020

The 5th Latin American Humanist Forum may be the most important forum in a generation. It arrives in the middle of a planetary pandemic that is affecting billions of people and paralyzing everything from transportation to the economy. The first Humanist Forum was held in 1993 in Moscow, initiated by Silo, the Argentine thinker/writer who developed an approach to nonviolent social and personal transformation. In his opening talk at the Moscow forum, Silo said:

"The Humanist Forum has the objective of studying and establishing a position on the global problems of today's world. From this point of view, it is a cultural organization in a broad sense that is concerned with structurally relating the phenomena of science, politics, art and religion. The Humanist Forum makes freedom of conscience and ideological unprejudiced the indispensable

condition for work in the understanding of the complex phenomena of the contemporary world."

The proposal of New Humanism is more relevant now than just a few years ago. Nonviolence in all aspects could become an alternative to the present set of values and structures that have been imposed by the North. Latin America should take the lead in launching a nonviolent cultural revolution.

Latin America needs to break free from its master, the White-West, which has been imposing its imposing political control, and with it its violent and selfish values, from Mexico to Chile. We saw it not long ago in Bolivia with the removal of Evo Morales by coup. The continent needs to be able to stand on its own two feet, without having to obtain support from the U.S. or Europe. People should stop immigrating north, amplifying the problems in their own countries and being used for political maneuver and cultural degradation. There is no proof that immigration resolves poverty, which itself was created by capitalist domination. Instead, a solution such as Universal Basic Income should be studied and developed as soon as possible, shifting the economic model through redistribution of financial resources to the general population.

Latin America has everything needed to develop itself and can flourish very rapidly; the difficulty is mostly in inertia, in the weight of the past. It is time to focus on the creation of a cultural identity that can generate strength and open the future by adopting a unifying image for all Latin America. This proposal goes beyond a political strategy, a tac tical alliance, or a so-called new development project. People need to connect at a much deeper level, to go beyond national politics, the flag, or the sport team, and really look at what these communities have in common. What is it that makes Latino culture different from other cultures? What are the best qualities of their people, and also the weaknesses that need to be addressed? If Latin America doesn't protect its Amazon forest, for example, no one else will. If Latin Americans do not cherish the unparalleled biodiversity of the Galapagos for human evolution someone else will steal it.

Latin Americans already have many successes and accomplishments to build upon. The Cuban experience in education in the 60's was very powerful, elevating the quality of life of millions of people. Today no one can deny the contribution to the world of the Cuban doctors, who came directly out of this educational process.

The strength and experience of the indigenous culture should be a model for building this new civilization. Recall how, just a few weeks ago, the Bolivian peoples regained political power in their country by way of democratic mobilization.

Latin America is, and has been for many decades, a Nuclear Free Zone. It would set an important example if every country of the continent were to ratify the new international treaty to ban nuclear weapons that will be entering into force in January 2021, making nuclear weapons illegal under international law forever. And all Latin American countries should follow the model of Costa Rica, who since 1949 has abolished its military, instead relying on the strength and techniques of nonviolence to resolve its conflicts.

We also have to acknowledge the Colombians achievement in signing a historic peace agreement after over 50 years of deadly civil war, and the ongoing process in Chile to rewrite the constitution established during the Pinochet military dictatorship.

As we can see, the continent is not without its share of extraordinary experiences and resources. Just last year, Pressenza partnered with China Global Television Network (CGTN) to produce a documentary "They Sense It Will Be Dawn," highlighting the work of avant-garde Latin American women who are applying science and technology towards the social and environmental good. The movie challenges the old concept of Latin machismo and the hegemony of the West in research and reveals a developing cultural partnership between China and Latin America.

There will be no Universal Human Nation until all cultures have matured, and feel the need to get together in an ambit of cooperation, exchange and coordination. Let this forum be a pioneer in that direction.

72nd Anniversary of the Universal Declaration of Human Rights

12/09/2020

December 10, 2020 marks the 72nd anniversary of the adoption of the United Nations' Universal Declaration of Human Rights (UDHR). The document is a powerful, and hopeful, testimony to the belief that all people on our planet should have access to fundamental human rights, including protection under the law, freedom of thought and expression, the right to an education, and the right to an adequate standard of living. It is difficult this year to imagine a joyful celebration of this milestone event, given the worldwide challenges presented by the COVID-19 pandemic. According to Feeding America, the largest American hunger relief organization, more than 50 million people will experience food insecurity this year in the U.S., the world's wealthiest country. "Across Latin America and the Caribbean, millions of the most vulnerable students may not return to school," said Bernt Aasen, UNICEF Regional Director for Latin America and the Caribbean. "For those without computers, without internet, or even without a place to study, learning from home has become a daunting challenge."

The pandemic has become a magnifying glass that highlights the gap between the aspirations of the declaration itself and the situation experienced today by people on the ground. The main challenge for this declaration, as opposed to previous advancements like universal education or the abolition of slavery, is that, as strong as it is, it is not a legally binding document. It was created, instead, as a reference to be followed and applied country by country. But here is the question: how many countries have changed their own constitutions to adopt the principles in this document? How many international institutions have embraced this declaration? Sadly, very few.

For example, let's look at Article 1: *All human beings are born free and equal in dignity and rights. They are endowed with reason and conscience and should act towards one another in a spirit of brotherhood.* If this article was universally applied, many police departments in the U.S. would be in big trouble. Only 110 law enforcement officers nationwide have been charged with murder or manslaughter in an on-duty shooting — despite the fact that 1,000 people are fatally shot by police annually, according to a database maintained by The Washington Post. Furthermore, only 42 officers have been convicted. And many of those convictions ended up being for a lesser offense — only five of these officers were convicted of murder (and did not have the conviction overturned). When will the U.S. Department of Justice be adopting the UDHR?

Imagine if the World Trade Organization applied the UDHR before it established trade agreements between countries; the world will be a very different place today. And we would witness a sea of transformations for millions of people if corporations and economic entities around the globe were to implement Article 23:

1. *Everyone has the right to work, to free choice of employment, to just and favorable conditions of work and to protection against unemployment.*
2. *Everyone, without any discrimination, has the right to equal pay for equal work.*
3. *Everyone who works has the right to just and favorable remuneration ensuring for himself and his family an existence worthy of human dignity, and supplemented, if necessary, by other means of social protection.*
4. *Everyone has the right to form and to join trade unions for the protection of his interests.*

As for education, Massachusetts passed the first compulsory school law in 1852 and by 1918, all American children were required to attend at least elementary school. Currently, the City of New York spends 33% of its budget on education and is legally obliged to accommodate any child requesting to be enrolled. Similar policies were adopted in many countries around the world and today UNESCO, with 193 member states, is leading efforts towards Universal Education. It may be our largest success at implementing a Universal Human Right and has been a very interesting demonstration effect.

In light of the challenges we are facing in a post-COVID world, perhaps Universal Basic Income (UBI) can be seen as the next human right to fight for. Just last week, World Food Program (WFP) chief David Beasley predicted that 2021 would likely be "the worst humanitarian crisis year since the beginning of the United Nations" 75 years ago, adding that, for a dozen countries, famine is "knocking on the door." In our society, no one can live without economic resources, and yet most people don't even have sufficient resources to look after themselves or their families. UBI would provide everyone with a minimum guaranteed income. Like the sentiment expressed in the UDHR, the basic tenet of UBI is that any economic system should be at the service of everyone's wellbeing, and not the other way around.

Hopefully, the enormous necessities of this time will help us to realize that there is much more security in adopting the UDHR than in continuing to spend vast energy and resources on immoral military budgets. Will the White-West — the so-called "developed world"– have the necessary leadership to shrink its military budgets and establish the betterment of all as a priority, as it did previously with education? It is not a question of creativity or new ideas, but rather a question of putting the human being as the central value and concern. May the Universal Declaration of Human Rights provide us with the roadmap to our first truly human society.

California State of Mind

12/21/2020

On November 1, the seven-day average for new COVID-19 cases in California was 4,183; on December 17 it was 38,774. The California Department of Public Health announced 379 COVID-19 deaths on December 17, the state's highest one-day total yet, shattering the prior record of 293 set the day before. More than 22,000 Californians have died from COVID-19 so far this year. In addition, 2020 has seen the state's largest wildfire season in modern history, with more than 4 million acres of land burned to date.

For almost 200 years, California has played a fundamental role in shaping American culture, from the 1849 Gold Rush, to the development of Hollywood, to the current dominance of Silicon Valley. "California Dreaming" created the allegory of a paradise on earth, a place where anyone could become rich and successful. The state in many ways has defined the ideal of the modern human being, with their array of gadgets, their obsession with fame and celebrity, and their pursuit of personal happiness. California epitomizes individualism: promoting car ownership over public transport, the house over apartment living, and the dream of having one's own business (started in the garage) or becoming famous at any cost.

This egocentric state of mind has created a disconnect with our environment, with our social fabric, and our society at large. Our individualism is so strong that we have lost the capacity to respond to common problems. One of the 12 Principles of Valid Action outlined by Silo says **"Things are well when they move together, not in isolation."** California and most of the Western world have been paying very little attention, if any, to "moving together" and instead have focused their energy and resources on staying "isolated," with the belief that that will make us more secure and less dependent. But the illusion of the self-made person is over.

As an example, people are concerned about when they will personally get the vaccine but, to really stop the pandemic's spread more than 70% of the population will need to be vaccinated. How to get to that 70% milestone should be everyone's current concern. Another example is obesity. Overall, 13% of the world's adult population was obese in 2016. The worldwide prevalence of obesity nearly tripled between 1975 and 2016. It's not an isolated issue, and asking people to follow some diet is not a solution.

And the climate change clock is clicking, requiring us to adjust our lifestyle. Remember: "Things are well when they move together, not in isolation."

Are corporations working to help people economically during this huge crisis? Can the U.S. Congress overcome its partisan divisions in order to pass important legislation? Will the military agree to reduce its own enormous budget so that the government can better help civilians in need?

Most of our present challenges are human made and could be transformed if we are ready to transform ourselves. Understanding that "things are well when they move together, not in isolation" is a good place to start modifying our belief system and re-organizing our priorities. A plane on the runway may be ready to fly, but if each of its motors starts running at a different speed or rotating in different direction, takeoff will never happen. What each one of us does is very important for ourselves and for everyone else.

January 6, 2021

01/28/2021

Over the past few months, I have written 13 articles on social issues that have arisen from what I call the culture of the "White-West." Then, January 6th happened. The Hill published an article a few days later titled "Pelosi says rioters chose their 'whiteness' over democracy," and she is right, but no one wants to address the race issue and the mainstream prefers to label it a political matter. The white man's motto is relatively simple and has been the same for centuries: to expand and maintain power through violence. Democracy, freedom, and the pursuit of happiness have been used as sophisticated justification for the use of violence in all its forms.

Today, we offer a new motto for our white friends: "Do everything possible to stop the spread of violence." A *Civil White Movement* is needed to transform this culture and take responsibility for centuries of colonialism, slavery, segregation, incarceration, militarism and poverty. We can start by repairing twice over the damage already done. We will no longer justify violence but will continue to educate, clarify, raise awareness, empower, and humanize. We will continue adding to the demands for public policies that protect, prevent and repair. At the economical level, we will support Universal Basic Income to ease and reduce the economical violence generated by the concentration of capital in very few hands. Reparations for slavery has been fiercely discussed in the United States since Union Army Gen. William Tecumseh Sherman promised 40 acres and a mule to 4 million freed slaves in 1865; it is a promise that is long overdue and needs to be met. At the political level, we need to expand voting rights as far and wide as possible, making our democracy as direct and inclusive as possible and making sure that minorities and people of color have access to all forms of power. In the same way we have used violence against each other, we have been violent against our own environment and we need to do everything possible to slow climate change. We will need to support the treaty to ban nuclear weapons, to reduce our enormous military budgets, to demilitarize the police, and to create institutions that focus on doing everything possible to stop the spread of violence.

These proposals are great and valid, but they are not enough. Something also needs to happen at the personal level, not just at the social. Change needs to happen in the depths of our consciousness and within our hearts. How do I respond to violence? Do I really believe that violence is not the solution? Violence manifests in many forms — hate, revenge, imposing your beliefs or your way of life, discrimination, the economic exploitation of people. In conclusion, we can all benefit by meditating on the following recommendation from "The Path" section of Silo's Message:

"Learn to treat others in the way that you want to be treated. Learn to surpass pain and suffering in yourself, in those close to you, and in human society. Learn to resist the violence that is within you and outside of you."

The Great Divorce of the Century

02/13/2021

The COVID pandemic has pushed the close-knit relationship between work and money towards a bitter divorce.

Millions lost their jobs and their money, some kept their jobs and their money, and still others made even more money without doing much. This situation didn't start with the pandemic, but it became more 'in your face' and it has created a social disaster, with hour-long lines at food pantries.

In the U.S. alone, 20 million people lost their jobs almost overnight. If you were working in a restaurant, a cultural institution, a club, or a theater, you were out of luck, out of work and without any income. If you were working in a job that allowed for remote work, however, you got to keep working, and the money kept rolling in. As it turns out, many of the people in lower wage work lost their jobs, while most of those earning higher wages kept theirs, and, in some cases, even saw their assets rise during the pandemic. Where is the fairness in that? No modern society should be developed with this type of structure.

On top of that, we still have a crazy system where most peoples' health insurance is linked to their work. So in the middle of one of the worst health crises in a century, many of the 20 million people who lost their jobs also lost their access to health insurance.

For centuries work has been accepted as the main distributor of wealth, either as compensation for time worked or through payment for objects produced. It's clear today, however, that work doesn't have the force nor capacity to really redistribute the growing concentration of capital. Household incomes have grown only modestly in this century, and household wealth has not returned to its pre-recession levels. Economic inequality, whether measured through the gaps in income or wealth between richer and poorer households, continues to widen, and it is anticipated that the post-pandemic economy will only exacerbate this trend (it is being described as K-shaped – the top half will keep going up while the bottom half will trend down). Income growth in recent decades has slanted steadily toward upper-income households: some 82% of money generated in 2017, according to Oxfam, went to the richest 1% of the global population, while the poorest half saw no increase at all. Here in the US, the middle class, which once comprised the clear majority of Americans, is fast shrinking.

The answer to this, we are told, is to invest more. During the 2008 crisis, however, millions of people who had worked hard for decades saw their pensions and retirement savings vanish overnight in the stock market. The work had been done but the money was gone.

And yet listen to any standard politician, be they Democrat, Republican, or even Independent, and you will hear the popular mantra of "jobs, jobs, jobs," as if that is the solution to everything. This allows them, after being elected, to justify increased military spending, polluting factories, and obscene corporate tax breaks, all in the name of "creating jobs." This is the tactic being used against Native Americans to push them off their sacred lands so they can build oil pipelines. And for all their talk about the importance of work, these politicians do little on behalf of workers' rights, which are being eroded year by year, and instead allow corporations to have more and more influence on workplace policy.

In reality, the notion of work is all about control. About controlling you and your behavior, what you can do and cannot do, what time to start and when to finish, what you can wear, when you can take a break or go on vacation. In some places, every few years they expect you to move, from city to city or country to country. And now, in this new "gig economy," you can be your own boss, with no capital, no clients and no strategy, just a serviceman to a corporation on a day to day basis – all without "being employed."

In a free society people should be able to spend their time and energy doing something that has meaning for them. They should be engaged in working together to build the kind of society we all aspire to. If you are really interested in moving our world forward, interested in helping the development of the human being, this is your issue. W need to move beyond this debilitating relationship between work and money. This divorce will have enormous consequences for our lives and the society at large. Imagine not having to spend 40 years waiting for retirement so you can start living.

We need to break the basic conditioning of birth, education, work and retirement. There is no natural law underlying this cycle. Our contribution to this world starts at the minute of our birth, when we become a human being. If we want our society to evolve, we can't keep spending the majority of our time, energy, and emotions doing something meaningless. We should be able to offer what we have, develop our best qualities, and open ourselves to learn, to love, to build, to discover, to share, and to imagine a new world.

We will have to redefine almost everything. What is the meaning of life, what is freedom, what is education? Imagine spending 15 years in school learning to respond to one question only: What is the contribution that I really want to make to this world?

I will let you respond to that question and, please, don't worry so much about money.

The Texas Climate and Energy Phenomena

02/18/2021

As millions of people in the South find themselves without power for a third day due to record-breaking winter storms, some have wondered why Texas isn't turning to other states for help.

To answer this, there are two important points to take in consideration, one about the electrical grid and other about climate change.

Let's start with the electrical grid. Texas, unlike the rest of the country, has its own electrical grid that is not connected to other states; 90% of the state's power supply is connected to a grid entirely within state lines. Texas has an independent grid because after the 1935 Federal Power Act, which gave the federal government authority to regulate power companies engaged in interstate commerce, Texas power companies got together and agreed not to sell power outside of the state, allowing them to avoid federal regulation. Almost 100 years later, nothing has changed as libertarians and rightwing politicians have maintained this absurd situation.

It's ironic that the state most identified with energy (oil production) is now without any electrical power. Can you imagine, in 2021, being without electricity for three days? No power for your phone, TV, computer, refrigerator, boiler, heater, cable modem, wifi, tablet, stove, coffee machine, toaster, microwave, lights, washing machine, clock, dryer, speakers...the list goes on.

As Texas and other parts of the country shelter in place and brace for a second wave of winter storms, some are questioning what role climate change played on these extreme weather patterns across the country. Chris Gloninger, a meteorologist with NBC10 Boston, explained the the connection in this way: *"There are waves in the jet stream and because of climate change and the warmer air in the Arctic and the largely ice-free Arctic sea, those waves are able to go far south. So places like Alaska or Iceland, which today is in the low 40s, are warmer than places like Texas, Louisiana or Oklahoma. That's why we're seeing these extremes."*

Today, Texas is faced with two societal concepts that are absolutely obsolete. The first is of the individual society that doesn't need any connection to or coordination with the Federal or International level, besides, that is, the "normal" business transactions of the oil market. This white-male egocentric individualism is dead and has no future. The second concept is the belief that climate change is not real and/or does not concern them. If they want to avoid a repeat of what is happening now, the state needs to modify its infrastructure in order to be prepared for future climatic change-related crises (changes in sea level, extreme temperature, clean water shortages, etc). It will have also to push the oil companies to become green energy companies. For this to happen, a profound transformation of its political landscape is required, something as strong as climate change itself. It is time to fire the political demagogues who have created this unimaginable situation.

I can't imagine what Texans are facing right now. but I definitely can imagine what they can do tomorrow to create a different future.

The Root of Violence in the United States Lies in the White Community

02/21/2021

Not long ago, Waging Nonviolence published an article entitled "The roots of revolutionary nonviolence in the United States are in the Black community." The article covered the process, starting in the 1930's, of African-Americans who traveled to India to learn about Gandhi's philosophy on nonviolence — a philosophy that was, of course, later developed in the U.S. during the Civil Rights movement and most famously embodied by MLK.

Since, then, many things have changed for the Black community, including having a Black American twice elected as President. But the situation today with the COVID pandemic paints a very sad picture. On February 2, a headline in USA Today proclaimed "The U.S. lost a whole year of life expectancy – and for Black people, it's nearly 3 times worse," underlining the gap that still exists in this country between whites and many people of color. The latter make up the majority of our front line, essential, retail, and delivery workers, those having to face COVID-19 directly. Many of them also live in multi-generational households, presenting challenges for social distancing and quarantining. The primary challenge now for communities of color is access to the vaccine. "My concern now," says Dr. Fola May, a UCLA physician and health equity researcher, "is if we don't vaccinate the population that's highest-risk, we're going to see even more disproportional deaths in Black and brown communities."

We can see the vaccination rollout as the highest example of structural and systemic discrimination. Vaccine research and production is in the hands of private corporations, accessible to those with the greatest ability to pay. And states' immunization plans are using technology as a filter: a person has to spend hours online, day after day, trying to get an appointment, which then could be canceled a day before. Let me ask you, who has the time, energy, and technological access for this?

The White-West has created these type of structures for centuries, making sure that white people stay in power. The financial structure is built on the same model as the vaccine implementation. A minority control the capital, then develop private structures for research and productions, which are then connected to a very complicated distribution/access system. It is as complicated for someone of color to get the vaccine as it is to gain access, for example, to financing for a house.

The White-West can't keep being the VIP of the world. Simply put, their problem is universality. For them, nothing can be for everyone, because if it's for everyone, then no one can control it. The U.S. Constitution begins with "We the People," a universal concept, yet we still keep in place an abstract form of democracy, with rules set up to make sure that not everyone can vote, leaving many of the "people" without any voice or representation.

The Biden administration claims to be working on immigration legislation that will legalize 10 million undocumented immigrants, mainly from Mexico and South America. But the question is: why has so little been done over so long a time? It is because immigration is not really about immigration, but about race. It is about keeping people of color out of the U.S. Our previous president expressed this sentiment very clearly during his campaign, using the allegory of a border wall with Mexico. That image gave him his win. The White-West needs the courage to call a racist racist, and stop trying to confuse the issue by giving it another name.

The problem is not the vaccine but its distribution. The problem is not money, but the concentration and control of it. The problem is not about education, but about the lack of universal access. The problem is not with politics, but with politicians trying to stay in power at any cost.

In this moment, the choice for the White-West is either to intentionally reject a belief in violence or to watch the continued downfall of our society. "We the People" has to be applied universally, as therein lies the future of humanity.

From National to Transnational Threat, the White-West is on the Move

02/23/2021

Attorney General nominee Merrick Garland's confirmation hearing testimony before the Senate Judiciary Committee was very significant, given the present moment. During his opening statement, Garland addressed the historical challenges faced by communities of color and the continual threat posed by the concentration of power within the white community:

"In conversations that I have had with many of you before this hearing, you have asked why I would agree to leave a lifetime appointment as a judge. I've told you that I love being a judge, but I have also told you that this is an impor-

tant moment for me to step forward because of my deep respect for the Department of Justice and for its critical role of ensuring the rule of law. Celebrating DOJ's 150th year reminds us of the origins of the Department, which was founded during Reconstruction in the aftermath of the Civil War to secure the civil rights that were promised in the 13th, 14th and 15th Amendments. The first Attorney General appointed by President Grant to head the new Department led it in a concerted battle to protect black voting rights from the violence of white extremists, successfully prosecuting hundreds of cases against white supremacist members of the Klu Klux Klan. Almost a century later, the Civil Rights Act of 1957 created the Department's Civil Rights Division with a mission to uphold the civil and constitutional rights of all Americans, particularly some of the most vulnerable members of our society. That mission, on the website of the Department's Civil Rights Division, remains urgent because we do not yet have equal justice. Communities of color and other minorities still face discrimination in housing, in education, in employment and in the criminal justice system, and they bear the brunt of the harm caused by pandemic, pollution, and climate change. 150 years after the Department's founding, battling extremist attacks on our democratic institutions also remains central to the Department's mission."

Not to think this issue is one faced solely by the U.S., last Monday United Nations Secretary-General Antonio Guterres, addressing the U.N. Human Rights Council, warned that white supremacy and neo-Nazi movements are becoming a "transnational threat" and have exploited the coronavirus pandemic to boost their support. U.N. High Commissioner for Human Rights Michelle Bachelet is to report to the council on March 18 on systemic racism worldwide against people of African descent. This global inquiry was launched after George Floyd's death in Minneapolis last May after a white police officer knelt on his neck for nearly nine minutes.

It is not a time for courageous people to let their guard down. Global systemic discrimination is much more organized than it has been for a long time. Churches are playing a role in dividing people as well.

A few months ago, Pope Francis expressed his concern about racist attitudes among some within his own church. "There are circles and sectors that present themselves as ilustrados (enlightened) — they sequester the proclamation of the gospel through a distorted reasoning that divides the world between 'civilized' and 'barbaric,'" he said in a November 2020 interview. "They consider a large part of the human family as a lower-class entity, unable to achieve decent levels in spiritual and intellectual life."

Of course, these positions are describing extreme situations, in special communities, but these "small" movements are supported and connected to a much larger community of people who share these views. Doing a few rounds of "diversity trainings" will not address the issue. The white community, my community, needs to stand up and be vocal against racism and discrimination wherever it appears. We can't just let others do the job for us.

Humanizing the World vs Going Back to Normal

04/01/2021

After months of waiting, the highspeed vaccination train is finally leaving the station, and hopefully, soon, they'll be room for everyone on board. It is perhaps the first time in history that every human being on our planet has faced the same phenomenon simultaneously. The worldwide scale of this pandemic has redesigned borders and is testing our society at its foundation. It has shown the efficiency of the scientific community, who, given simple guidelines, in less than a year came up with multiple vaccines on different continents. At the opposite end, we are watching the collapse of the political sphere, where there has been almost no international coordination, insufficient support for the medical community, and a disastrous level of miscommunication regarding the virus and the vaccination implementation. Even worse are the corporations, which are basically sitting out the pandemic, waiting to steal anything they can while at the same time concentrating their power even more, like vultures feasting on weakened prey.

Here we are in front of this peculiar situation, with a vaccination process that, day by day, gains momentum and a mainstream media campaign that promises we are soon going "back to normal." (In his first major speech, President Biden bragged "The U.S. could return to a kind of normal by the Fourth of July.") This is crazy: no one wants to go back to normal, when "normal" means violence against women, families living in poverty, meaningless jobs, polluted air and water, segregated schools, racist religions, immoral military budgets, and corrupt politicians. This "normal" is blocking humanity's evolutionary process of surpassing pain and suffering and is undermining the construction of a diverse and nonviolent universal human nation. Here are few synonyms for normal: usual, standard, typical, common, ordinary, conventional, habitual, expected, boring, mechanical. I ask you, who wants to live in a normal society?

People of the world didn't endure this pandemic and undergo all of these troubles for nothing. Everyone is aware that things have to change everywhere. It is the moment to humanize the earth, an opportunity to grasp a new perspective on life and to forge a new image of our collective future. The relationship between cultures needs to be humanized, corporations and economic systems need to be humanized, social participation and political representation need to be humanized, our relationship with nature and our planet needs to be humanized. The meaning of our lives needs to be humanized.

As we have seen with this pandemic, and before that with climate change, the world is one and interconnected. Now, if only people would feel one and interconnected. Our force is our universality; everything has to be for everyone. We can't vaccinate some and not all. We can't have some working for climate change and others polluting like madmen. We can't have some nations with food bombing others with starving communities. We can't have a few countries with nuclear weapons and others bullied like kids on a playground. We can't have some families with multiple homes and others living on the street. We can't have some children with laptops and wifi connection and others without even lunch. We are done trying to find a piecemeal solution, giving a little to some and none to others. We can no longer let the System play its "division" politics. "Divide ut regnes" (divide, in order to reign) was a Roman practice of relocating groups with longstanding grudges in close proximity to one another so that their constant fighting would keep them from collaborating to overthrow Roman rule. It is still the prevalent governing tactic today, and we must be vigilant to prevent it from being used against us.

We are the front-line workers of humanity's future, fighting against apathy and nihilism, striving for converging diversity, organizing against injustice through active-nonviolence, and promoting equal rights and equal opportunities for all human beings. We will need everyone's energy, ideas, and effort if we are going to take advantage of this opportunity and, hopefully, finally, never go back to normal.

George Floyd Facing the White-West

04/01/2021

The trial of Derek Chauvin, the police officer charged with murder and manslaughter in George Floyd's death, started this week. Before the trial began, Floyd family attorney Ben Crump blasted the idea that the trial would be a tough test for jurors. "We know that if George Floyd was a white American citizen, and he suffered this painful, tortuous death with a police officer's knee on his neck, nobody, nobody, would be saying this is a hard case."

In his testimony, Donald Williams, a former wrestler, said he yelled to Chauvin that he was cutting off Floyd's blood supply. Williams recalled that Floyd's voice grew thicker as his breathing became more labored, and he eventually stopped moving. "From there on he was lifeless," Williams said. "He didn't move, he didn't speak, he didn't have no life in him no more on his body movements."

The defense attorney, Eric Nelson, disputed that Chauvin was to blame for Floyd's death. "Floyd, 46, had none of the telltale signs of asphyxiation and he had fentanyl and methamphetamine in his system," Nelson said. He said Floyd's drug use, combined with his heart disease, high blood pressure and the adrenaline flowing through his body, caused a heart rhythm disturbance that killed him.

We have already seen that hundreds of similar cases finished with either no verdict or a light sentence for the police officers charged. No one yet knows the outcome of the Floyd trial but, independent from the result, we know it will not truly address the issue at hand — hate and white supremacy.

The jurors will not be given any insight into Chauvin's life, what type of school he went to, who his parents were, what neighborhood he lived in, what motivated him to become a cop, what political party he was part of, or what church he belonged to. This is not the Nuremberg trial (as it should be) but rather a black family pitted against a policeman, within a judicial system shown over and over to protect the institution of the police. Justice here is the application of "law and order," and is not about to address the discrimination of one race against another, the underlining motivation behind Floyd's killing.

Instead, the white man will hide behind his institutions, keeping his supremacy in check. The president of New York City's police union, Patrick J. Lynch, gave his union's endorsement to President Trump in August 2020, saying "Mr. President, we are fighting for our lives out there." Nearly 90% of the union's' leaders — officers, trustees, financial secretaries — are white, and even more are men, according to the New York Times. If this is the situation in NYC, we can imagine what it's like in the rest of the country.

There is nothing new here; all of this happened for decades, if not centuries, before. Renée Ater has created a memorial page on honor of those unarmed black and brown people killed by the police, sheriff deputies, and security guards. You can also visit the #SAY THEIR NAMES page and see their faces. These are heartbreaking lists, much too long for any human heart to read.

The real question is, if Black Lives Matter and the Civil Rights movement have not transformed this hate and discrimination, what will? The real issue is that white culture needs to change, needs to transform itself, needs a cultural revolution. We need to replace hate and discrimination with "treat other as you want to be treated," replace competition with cooperation, replace law and order with peace and justice, replace individualism with universalism, replace rich and poor with valid actions and happiness. We need to replace second amendment of the U.S. constitution with Article 2 of the Declaration of Human Rights and we need everyone's cooperation to do it. Teachers on Long Island, Staten Island, and in every white neighborhood should transform their curricula, artists should be standing against discrimination without fear of losing their fans, the media should stop mediatizing violence and focus on human development and process in all fields (science, medicine, economic, common goods, democracy, technology, cultures, environment). The churches should stop becoming political machines keeping a minority in power and corporations should understand their responsibility to transform the disparity between rich and poor.

As we don't know the final judgment in Chauvin's trial, we also don't know what will happen to the White-West. Will it be smart enough to adapt and transform itself, or will it fall like the Egyptians or Romans? This trial, unfortunately, will not answer any of these questions and real justice will not be served.

From George Floyd to a Cultural Reconciliation Process

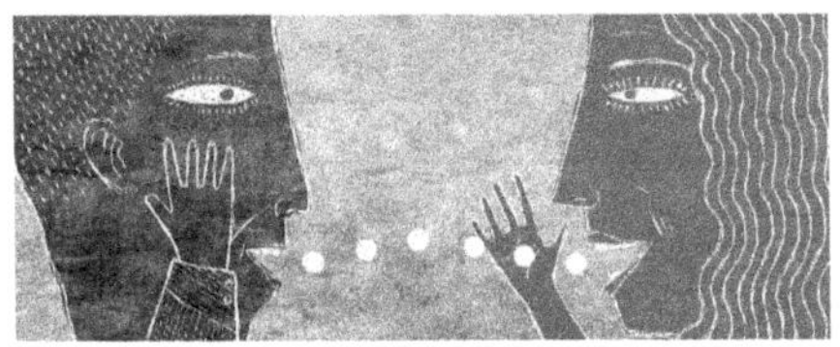

04/16/2021

Daunte Wright's death on April 11 in Brooklyn Center, 10 miles south of Minneapolis, came as the city was already on edge, in the middle of the trial of former police officer Derek Chauvin for the death of George Floyd last May. Anticipating unrest, in remarks to the nation President Biden stressed there is "absolutely no justification" for looting and violence. "Peaceful protest is understandable," he said. "And the fact is that we do know that the anger, pain and trauma that exists in Black community in that environment is real – it's serious, and it's consequential. But that does not justify violence." The problem with this sentiment is that you can't just remove "looting and violence" without replacing it with something. You can't denounce violence without replacing it with nonviolence.

The Floyd and Wright murders are one aspect of racism against Blacks; the COVID pandemic gave us striking picture of the precarious situation of many people of color in our country. The current vaccination process has highlighted existing structural problems that favors the white community, who were also less affected by the pandemic than Black and Latinx communities. Similar structures are at play in education, the military, and the economic system. And the Asian-American community has been the target of hate attacks across the country, the result of racist propaganda that has tried to paint COVID as an "Asian" virus.

The time has come for the U.S. to start its own cultural reconciliation process, based on experiences of peace processes carried out in other parts of the world (Ireland, Kosovo, South Africa, Colombia) and addressing cultural tensions between "minorities" and the dominant "White-West." The violence against minorities needs to be studied from diverse perspectives and experiences. A cultural reconciliation process would not just look at the present moment but would go back to slavery and the era of colonialism, and it would look at the development of White-Christian hegemony and the notion of second and third-class citizenry, which still exists today.

Implementing any successful peace and reconciliation process, however, would require both sides to recognize the urgency and the need for such a process. The two sides need to acknowledge that the conflict exists, that violence won't resolve it, and that nothing that has been done until now has provided a solution.

The current administration looks at the situation the same way as previous administrations, without any real understanding of the root of violence in U.S. society. They see the violence as a kind of "collateral damage" of a great system, not so good but certainly unavoidable.

The illusion of the "great society" goes along with the illusion of cultural white supremacy. We will be ready for a cultural reconciliation process when these illusions vanish from the dark side of our consciousness and we undertake the transformation of our belief system.

Principle 11

"It does not matter in what faction events have placed you what matters is for you to understand that you have not chosen any faction."

from "The Inner Look"by Silo

Epilogue

On September 3, 2021, ICAN, the 2017 Nobel Peace Prize winner, released a briefing report titled *Racism, Colonialism, and Nuclear Weapons.* In it they document how international security priorities have long been dominated by the White Western elite, in particular around the development of nuclear weapons. "Racism," it reads, "is at the core of fundamental assumptions about nuclear weapons policy: who is permitted to develop nuclear weapons, who is listened to and on whom the United States has considered dropping its nuclear weapons."

Two weeks later, on September 16, the US and the UK signed an agreement to provide nuclear submarine technology to Australia, strongly increasing pressure on China. After getting out of a messy 20 year war that destroyed Afghanistan, it seems the White-West is in need of a new enemy to feed its addiction.

What makes this stupidity even more enraging is that it is happening during a global pandemic of unprecedented proportions, with thousands dying every day and no clear end in sight. The "me-first" vaccination process has shown the White-West's corporate mindset; they miss the point of a *universal* vaccination campaign and are using irrelevant criteria such as intellectual property rights and profit to justify their immoral actions.

Finally, it's difficult to close this book without mentioning the role of the White-West on our environment. The White-West, is responsible for a large majority of the world's C02 emission despite representing only 14% of its population. Just this summer, we saw horrifying images of fires, flooding and drought. Hundreds of thousands, if not millions, of people were displaced, many died, and billions of dollars was lost in reconstruction costs.

These are perhaps the three greatest threats facing our planet today – nuclear war, the COVD pandemic, and catastrophe climate change. And yet is has become abundantly clear that the White-West mentality -- this out-of-date, misguided, self-centered view of the human being and of the world --- is not only largely responsible for them but also totally incapable of providing a coherent response.

Hopefully, the pressure produced by these crises will bring about important shifts in our beliefs and our system of values. We need to think and act from a different place. It is not enough anymore, for example, to "help" the poor and discriminated; it is time to challenge exploiters and discriminators, to make it clear that their actions are not acceptable. We need to go beyond defunding the police and defund our whole structure of discrimination and racism, to face it with courage, to look to ourselves in the mirror and acknowledge our responsibility.

The White-West has created its own version of reality, one built and subsequently maintained through violence, imposition, and exploitation. Violence has become so embedded in its way of operating that it pretends it's not there; instead of labeling the violence, it calls it "spreading democracy," "promoting economic development," or "stamping out terrorism." The first step toward any real change is for the White-West to recognize its dependence on violence in all its forms (physical, economic, racial, and psychological) in order to get what it wants. It must realize that violence has not and will not produce peace and security. To continue in this way has no exit, it will only lead to more violence and ultimately to its own destruction. Many civilizations have collapsed under the weight of their own violence, not able to recognize and correct the destructive direction in which they found themselves caught. And, personally, each of us must make a decision to renounce violence in our own lives. One should make a daily routine of studying violence in oneself: see it, touch it, work with it, transform it. Learn to give up control in order to save oneself.

The second step is related to that particular social, cultural, and political landscape in which the White-West was formed, and which still shapes its worldview today. While we cannot change the landscape of our past, and all the associations and structures that come with it, how interesting it would be to intentionally give charge to other images that relate to the future, images that align with the universal human nation that is taking shape. These images represent a new set of values – ones that prioritize cooperation over competition, people over money, diversity over monopoly. It is no longer viable to speak of progress for some people without progress for all humanity; it is becoming clearer that what impacts anyone on the planet impacts me as well. This is the evolution of things, and the sooner the White-West can understand this, the sooner it will see that it is in their best interest to share resources and power with all on the planet. Resisting will only extend the suffering we are seeing now.

The ICAN briefing report, while noting the role of the White-West in nuclear proliferation, also spoke to the important role that indigenous peoples and people of color have played at the forefront of the nuclear disarmament movement. It is a good reminder that while the White-West may often dominate the news, there are many other players who have been and are ready to continue making their contribution to our universal human nation. It's time we expand the platform.

Get on board and continue this discussion by sending your own testimony and point of view at: white-west.com

Acknowledgements

Let me start first by conveying my sincere gratitude to my dear friend Dennis Redmond, without whom it would have been impossible for me to publish any of these articles. Dennis is my editor-in-chief. He not only makes corrections and looks after spelling mistakes, but he also keeps the text flowing and in theme without changing the sense, the tone, or the dynamic of the piece. His closeness and support have made this book feasible.

Pressenza and my community of humanist friends have been crucial supports and good partners in this process. This is not the type of book that you do alone in your cave; this book is very social, it's about us, all of us, whether we like it or not, whether we agree or not. I totally understand that some of my friends do not see things the same way as me and this is what has reinforced my motivation to do this series of articles. It is not about convincing anyone but rather looking at our landscape through daily events, seeing what we value and why, recognizing who we trust and who we don't.

Finally, my thanks to my family for their patience, eternal support and profound kindness. As my wife Yolanda put it, "There is a lot of love here," and it's what makes it extraordinaire. Thank you.

David Andersson is a French-American who has been living in New York City for over 27 years.

A citizen journalist, photograph and publisher, David is currently the coordinator of Pressenza's New York bureau and host of the talk show *Face2Face*, broadcast on Youtube and Facebook.

His publishing experience starting in the 1980's with the operation of a neighborhood newspaper in Paris. During the 2000's he published a multilingual magazine called *DiverCity*, showcasing the growing cultural diversity of New York City and addressing the discrimination faced by the immigrant communities in Queens.

David was involved with the Occupy Movement and was a founding member of Occupy Queens.

Affiliated with the Humanist Party, David coordinated the New York Coalition to Expand Voting Rights (iVote NYC), for over 7 years. The goal of the coalition was to pass local legislation to grant the right to vote in municipal elections to all legal residents, regardless of citizenship status.

www.ingramcontent.com/pod-product-compliance
Ingram Content Group UK Ltd.
Pitfield, Milton Keynes, MK11 3LW, UK
UKHW020422250726
13067UKWH00007B/2773

9 780578 924182